Seven
INTO Even

Seven
INTO Even

JACQUELINE TURNER

MISFIT

ECW PRESS

Published by ECW PRESS
2120 Queen Street East, Suite 200, Toronto, Ontario, Canada M4E 1E2

LIBRARY AND ARCHIVES CANADA CATALOGUING IN PUBLICATION

Turner, Jacqueline, 1965–
Seven into even / Jacqueline Turner.

Poems.
ISBN 1-55022-746-7

1. Spenser, Edmund, 1522?-1599. Faerie queene.
2. Deadly sins—Poetry. I. Title.

PS8589.U7476S48 2006   C811'.6   C2006-903597-0

A misFit Book

Editor for the press: Michael Holmes / a misFit book
Cover and Text Design: Tania Craan
Cover Art: John Tonkin
Author photo: Brennan/Blake Kurchak
Typesetting: Mary Bowness
Printing: Marquis

This book is set in Fairfield

The publication of Seven Into Even has been generously supported by the Canada Council, the Ontario Arts Council, and the Government of Canada through the Book Publishing Industry Development Program.

DISTRIBUTION
CANADA: Jaguar Book Group, 100 Armstrong Ave.,
Georgetown, ON L7G 5S4

PRINTED AND BOUND IN CANADA

ECW PRESS
ecwpress.com

CONTENTS

BOOK 1

Constant Mind

You play words across technical pages
Your form constrained by hour and look
While hiding she pops forth with imaginary goldfish
That you definitely can't eat or maybe you can
You work three jobs fall asleep exhausted
To the sound of someone reading dark words
And dream of what abandoned coasts can offer

Antique Times

You brush dust off the surface where the TV used to sit
Wax nostalgic for half a second you might bite your lip
Forget remembering a breath at the back of your neck
Hands cupping your breasts from behind, no you have
Moved on into another cream-coloured room where
Your desire can be measured in typical terms like
Groceries and renovations and batteries for clocks
That have recently stopped

Strong Compulsion

Mine too: it should be reasonably confessed
Because you know what they say about confession
And my days are measured out by coffee and breakfast
Dropping off one boy and then the other: Jimi Hendrix
This morning and Deep Purple tomorrow today I'm craving
Leonard Cohen again and you can only listen to so much "Dear Heather"
Before your chest aches with the want of what you cannot have
Because you simply didn't choose it

Who First Should Be

Walking the handful of streets that make up Horseshoe Bay
Where the dog does her trick for the last tourists of the season
We forgot to rent a boat this summer or didn't have time
Forgot to plant the pots and read books instead while you
Contemplated a life ruined by reading or soap operas
We kept making up romantic pen names for future romances
Arguing to ourselves that it had to pay off in the end

Gentle Wise

Your blueness sparkles up the hill to Tantalus Park
Always wanting less than you need around the green
Corner while I keep linking words to desires without
The reach forward to grab your hand tightly because
I will not be known or seen: almost invisible and cryptic
Snake skin shedding that shimmery trace you pick up
And examine closely through the light

Running Sore

When the dark days hit answering the phone
Is an impossible task and your message about
The smell of the showers at the Y fizzures through
And even though I don't call back the smell
Conjures around the rest of the day and even though
I can't sleep tonight or any night my back relaxes
Into the worn sheets again

Fell Through Emptiness

When you couldn't breathe in labour for three whole days
My voice kept catching in my throat some financial panic
Yours came forth with a dream made manifest: a pocket,
A bundle, full of what joy obviously but refusing to be precious
About it still calm and frantic: you love small toes but don't
Like sleepless nights; intense substance here, you feel her weight
Against your once broken shoulder

BOOK 2

Disguise

you attend small ruptures when the routine of the day breaks apart you celebrate small interludes the sound of drums being played in a garage across the alley when he asks again if he can play the drums where you say where we live in a duplex and our neighbours probably already hate our dog being cat people and quite quiet but it only takes the buzz of the saw cutting down another tree or part of a tree or maybe just the top of a tree to make you realize you've forgotten to turn off the oven and soon the door will ping open you remember yourself at that age scrambling under the stairs to find the hook and the key letting yourself in and liking the quiet

Tract of Time

you caress the edge of each table, roughly, you aren't precious about it but still couldn't write the letter imagined at two in the morning to an uncle whose wife had died in one of the worst possible ways because almost no one would believe she was sick because believing she was sick would mean facing what was all around them the air and maybe what they put on their crops and how that made its way to her lungs filling them too full the day she died and if you could move back to the table where the pen is the paper you could go buy a card but cards are too cliche to make you/him feel better or flowers like she used to sew at the edges of coats or dresses or even towels even when she was sick and you should write that letter because you're always saying people don't know what you're thinking unless you tell them that you don't get what you want unless you ask for it until you sound like a caption for a fridge magnet in the worst of the Atwood novels

Suspended Dreadfully

you fail to understand why her partner may have left her or why it rains on the day you planned to go to the bike park or the beach or why sometimes a conversation about a friend with another friend reveals how you may have misjudged someone else and now you understand that it takes longer in Vancouver to make friends and you don't have to go back to your high school journal to see that some particular insecurities repeat themselves in contemporary structures that the structure (call it Vancouver) calls for or causes this repetition running your hands through the sand at Bachelor Bay and when you told your son that this day the day he was born was the happiest day he can't resist saying what about Blake was that your second happiest day

Things Present

you can finally attend to it outside the neighbour feeds the crows what looks like catfood and the biggest joke is that one can call the kids for lunch through the overgrown green or from atop the flat mossy roof where once there were cottages once no ferry no impending bog destroying overpass: a jewel a gem that now features the largest number of divorced people in the whole area so much so that people wondered if you were moving on your own there your husband is he moving too

Ambitious Minds

you become enamoured of wax seals on letters never sent or seldom
received the crisp potential of stacks of paper in the shop when a brisk
yellow bird becomes framed in the window and you have no idea of the
name thinking bird watching a ridiculous pursuit but still it sits sway-
ing on the branch in the wind occasionally shitting and peering around
red markings around the eyes you should write it down tell your dad in
a letter so he can look it up

Taking Odds

you know what to tell when she asks why she's still single or why she moves directly into a relationship after one broke up they both say it's habitual but more it's knowing how to show someone they're fabulous wrap their life up and give it back a present their blue eyes both penetrate no question running toward and away at the same time like in a dream when your Flintstone feet paddle the pavement furiously but you still can't get away

Not by Strong Hand Compelled

you always reached out to him when he was a raging kid and now he's happy and even tempered for the most part we reach through our own rage at being the youngest and try to appreciate his being the oldest checking our visceral responses to being punched playfully on the arm somewhat playfully we can't stand fighting anyway and veto the boxing classes suggesting pottery though falls on more than deaf ears or drama classes because of his great comic timing only demonstrated when almost no one is listening and never to be repeated on request

BOOK 3

by my life

tepid toes
reach across sheets
pear juice
dripping down
brownish yellow
where cocks
have withered
lightly now
penetration ceases
your grief
not being desired
hot breath
the way you
imagined or
the way you
were for
one heavy summer
one hot year
burning becomes
burden shouted
or whispered
ocean's edge
red pier

monster ready

dry gasp
seeks pale
tongue for
light licking
shack
all the way
heady humming
outloud for
whoever can hear

earnestly inquire

lean into
the new edge
built this year
or last
run fingers
or clasp
some smooth
small stream
people file behind
occasionally ask
how old
how long since when
first warning
ferry sounds
mountain refuse
echo

turn back to that place

funny how
a photo strip
of sand
balance water
log slips
becomes yoga
meditation well
fuck yoga
t-shirts take
certain risks
fashion frenetic
what to wear
so the weeds
won't catch
your feet
how about
a gingham
tube top
trains pass
refuse again
to wave

certain space

trace dimensions
always need
improving endless
revision edit
paint it red
please paint it
something because
beige is oppressive
sings an eerie tune
man that's annoying
like whistling in
the van first
in the morning
shrill beat
sure it shows talent
otherwise unexpressed
can't be that
supportive this early
please stop is
the best i can do

world's desired view

ride this cool expanse
clear water deep
where shallow rise
weeds hit edges
of mattresses
becomes putrid now
you spit smell gags
fall off and run
retch to the end
wonder: "reading dreams
like metaphors
like poetry"
if water is baptismal
yours has emerged
from clear to
shitty mess

much better

flat taste wails
no bright green
mouthwash can save
find your tremor
today your left
eye twitches lightly
come on
are you nervous
or should you learn
to breathe deeply
embrace your meditative
lack flat space
or no place
without so many people
even trees crowd
today thrust
green to the edge
slight fade to yellow
driving into
your very chest

BOOK
4

lust

lip to nipple's edge
tongue weighing lightly
or biting sharply
you come around
my hand

if i wanted to touch you lightly then the build up of angst asks me to
kiss you heavily our lips together smooth or biting the outer edge of
skin pressed together not perfectly taste of beer or stain of wine your
mouth explodes with yes of all the years we've spent together or days
apart where the white caress of hotel sheets holds us in their separate
grasps dry and gasping maybe somewhat guilty as our hands continue
to press the space between savouring the saturated moment where we
are and always wanting the crisp wetness of somewhere else

pride

you think you know
dull edges of my mind
thoughts as bright as
synapses firing or
colours where my sympathies
lie crunched together
you don't

if i showed you a bright picture splattered thickly with paint and you
shrugged it off or walked past without comment if you proclaimed my
neighbour's talent again: she's so this, she's so that, if i thought about
ripping your head off on the page but couldn't draw that well if i needed
excessive praise to talk for hours about that one line how great it looked
on the page how it leapt through the static to be heard precisely voice
husky or deep if i coveted that handful of words held it close my precious
until it fell away dry powder you sprinkle over the clothes in the back-
room laundromat

envy

i could never
like that never
wouldn't want to
anyway

in a neighbourhood where houses are coveted brushed to a bright sheen glossed over and over renovated and re-renovated but where you're never invited past the foyer unless it's a party, unless it's an event and no one just drops by for coffee can't even drag them in for a glass of wine when they drop off or pick up the kids got to get home and clean the house or the cleaners are coming in a neighbourhood like that it's weird to feel envy for what people have what they covet after a good day on the market, a great real estate buy wealth without much work not that you work hard anyway painting the wall red because you want it that way not because some designer told you this year it's fuchsia darling

gluttony

your creamy thighs
your chocolate eclair
smeared sweet
back of my throat

just can't get enough of just can't get enough of just can't get enough
ginger stings the back of my throat chocolate presses between my
tongue and the roof of my mouth a crisp glass of thick red wine drips
and gushes or a cold pot of beer my lips on a hot day sizzles crackles
but goes down smooth eventually and another and another and anoth-
er raspberry vodka and muddled lime mmmm or cheese dripping
thickly off the edges of crackers whipped cream straight out of the
aerosol can suffocating slightly the tip of my nose or the dark hit of
coffee with a milky tinge zing to stay awake with all night long

sloth

noon and i'm still
not dressed no
plans to either

languid heat presses my head back into the couch the book slips from
my grasp eyes heavy or languid heat presses my head into the sand
sunglasses shade and my eyes slip or languid heat presses my head
toward the desk jerking at the computer's edge or languid heat presses
my head into the cool of the refrigerator turning to caress my cheek icy
or languid heat presses my head into the cool of white sheets someone
has crisply ironed or languid heat presses my head into your inappro-
priate shoulder

greed

sharing is caring
kate said to blake
sharing is caring

hoarding your love, your lego into piles you gather it in rake it all
toward your chest: mine you said making your little voice go deep pick
one piece for yourself you whose space is always being invaded whose
towers are always getting knocked over before they're finished fate of
the youngest, i know, to never feel sure what you've built up carefully
won't be destroyed in one fell swoop, one perfectly timed kick to your
most vulnerable spot

anger

tree lined street
trees planted in rows
hanging off weeping willows

goddamn it don't swing on those christ get off now you'll break the
branches i thought i told you stop you little brat go to your room now
now and i don't want to see you and i don't want to see you and i don't
want to see you until you can bloody well apologize

BOOK
5

sunday

sunday's a sad day pit of the stomach a lurch against the way things should be even the family dinner when everyone's laughing around the tables pushed together your mother rushing to get all the food on the table sit down mom someone will inevitably say but she won't until it's all there and everyone else is almost done and you still feel alone lonelier than you've ever felt surrounded by the people who love you without thinking about it a glass of sweet white wine over the turkey sloshes as you push past the desire to analyze every second of it a baby bangs mashed potatoes against a tray or chews on a slipper before anyone notices pink satin dress flaring

monday

there always seems to be school on monday even now that you're an adult and the tables have turned you see a yellow school bus and you rush just in case all the good seats are taken "I don't like mondays" a song you discussed endlessly with lisa and where is she now on mondays you get the kids to school driving bleary as jimi hendrix blares beautifully like he always does he always did guitar rift like playing the strings of your veins

tuesday

never a good night for a reading people aren't gearing up yet an insular
sort of evening bath water running and running foam piled high your
elbow hits the tub hard wipe your hands on a towel so you can read
the new marlatt without getting it wet words rising up to meet your eye
you have found your place in language as you languish head at the
edge hair damp as words pop and then flow together

wednesday

why would we care inhaling deeply the relentless salt air or the bite of its raining again and the rain soaked us through and through because we forgot the umbrella again or we don't believe in umbrellas awkwardly banging into people on the street or we have never learned to use them properly lift or lower at precisely the right moment passing and plastic raincoats suffocate your skin shrink wrapped why not just get wet

thursday

crunches around the dream i had while you slept in my faraway bed
visiting my empty house my breath always at your neck never your lips
are you happy i kept saying in my dreamy voice are you really happy i
am now you whispered not wanting to wake all the others my hand on
your thigh lightly pressing like you can in dreams saying something like
because you are queen that sounds ridiculous when you play it back in
your morning mind knowing it came from reading spenser the night
before

friday

pours me a thick glass of red wine clink as anxiety sinks away pour me another and we start to talk faster and we feel freer to say whatever comes to mind without stopping another and we grow flirtatious a hand on an arm across the table another and we are witty at parties there's always something clever to say another and we are the most interesting people in the world another and we profoundly sigh seeing it all so clearly another and we solve global warming another and we know how to convince quebec to stay another and we are enraptured with our brilliance clothes falling to the floor

saturday

sleeps in no question reads and reads in bed until the kids get sick of
cartoons and come bouncing in pillows flying until someone gets hurt
and then the crying stretching making breakfast and bang the imperative
to do something to accomplish some task to justify the weekend the
lawn the laundry while the kids want to go to a movie or a ride to the
bike park a walk and pretty soon the sun hits the red chair lounging look-
ing out to the bay mmmm and it's time for a nap

BOOK
6

fashion/able

stick to styles liar
how to lip
file fleet
heels forever
gold or gold or
stock adopt
carried leather
green garbage
echo reactor
ecru bleeds
ought survey
before oust
creationist texture
out skirt current
size outside
pattern protrude
strip clever
note dance relation

fashionist/a

formidable flounce
hair slick
street seen
traffic slumber
pages flipped
cartesian control
pleasure card
flag eddy foam
zipper talk fringe
stale topics
lack reaction
outshot work related
retracts silk shot
tremulous bizarre
sequence vain
rude station out
weight fraction
calm frenzy

i/flower

lie lilac late
crisp frenetic proof
perceptual cross
cream rises
light crenate
prestige pearly
mnemonic lavender
reach acrete
sky coincide cloud
correlate down the road
frugal fingers
wrap around
town tone
stem strikes
wide mouth
sun or rain glint
globular precision
brown before
visions implicate
perceptible whack
scissors stuck
table leg bent

brooch/the subject

badge tone centre
pin weight of city
here or clasp rich
night market deal
deploy *it* in a perceptual
space to cross your neck
a jaunty, but modest assertion
the jab of territory utters
the subjectivity of the traveller
who passes through
with a whisper of chiffon
pulled tight though
to coincide with cable
to create some relationship
with the we of community
hollow where one decorative
stone lies missing an echo
of act or act act act

into/nation

correlative of *voice*
in state of excitement
like ideas in state of
excitement worn clearly
worn shoulder patch
accompanies perceptible
sign who passes through
flesh of longitudinal longing
no the body particular
fingers labia folds across
social contract first contact
meaning some different
bead necklace to each
worn lovingly at first
mimetic prestige inserts
historical documents
hair clips invariant with
utterances of visions
come here unctuous
sleeve come right
over here

citi/zen

another cosmopolitan
creates equilibrium
in its *natural* state
remember your membership
badge affix it here and here
band together remember
bar stools tip easily
subjectivity gets blurry
wow your makeup
shimmers with obligation
you've accumulated
quite a collection your
freshly waxed legs shine
you'd be at home everywhere
pink inhabits an urban experience
again when implications
coincide or subside
up your tree lined street

de/ploy

violence gets voice
from column into line
every high school classroom
has at least one camera
designed into effective action
jeans slung just to coincide
with certain predetermined
territory like that's so
grade nine hardcore
if stuffed into a garbage can
or folded into a locker
a reconnaissance trip
might be required some
jerk who knows how
to drive now might say
"did you see how mean
he was to her" in wooden
video voice before the
bleeding starts to run
over white t-shirts

BOOK 7

OR

MUTABILITY

They Together Run

her size: zero/*fat*

her loss: 40 pounds (and counting)

her stupid question: are you expecting?
          (oh no, it's just the way you're standing)

                                 her score: (a lifted chorus)
                              Britomart *withstood with courage stout,*
                      And them repaide againe with double more

guarding the bodily territory is full time exhausting
            this space: open for discussion
                      are you going to eat *that?*

the tone of her body vibrates
cries out for food, but only gets
sugarless gum and black coffee

                          . . . that stroke so cruell passage found,
                  That glauncing on her shoulder plate, it bit
                                     Vnto the bone

magazine colonizer
you're not model thin
but you could be

Her wisedome did admire, and hearkned to her loring

couldn't stick with the awesome abs class
hated pilates

Vppon her head she wore a Crowne of gold
To shew that she had a powre in things diuine

you're always reading why don't you go for a walk
or come watch TV with us

oh that's fabulous
it hides your hips
it makes you look thin

the social contraction
weighed down in the public domain
delivering (even virtually) more of the same

you don't quite look like the picture you posted

Whilest Fortune fauourd her successse in fight

your discourse doesn't get me hot
move further into the light
where i can see/seize your artifacts
ravish the *écrits* of your clit

(come on, pleasure is in exposure)

confess your excess
and all will be [insert contemporary diet plan here] well
after all, numbers don't lie, scales signal so what or so what now

obligatory concealment of the body
translates to satin, lace or sturdy cotton
fold egregious skin inside another skiff

Whom that proud Amazon subdewed had

    this interruption:
    (represents "the point where the insistence of
    the real forced an end to pleasure and where the
    pleasure found a way to surface despite the economy dictat-
    ed by the real")

or maybe i misread your intention
to be ravishing your tongue right there
signified some other kind of pleasure
as you lifted my belly

it felt real anyway

In which when as she him anew had clad
She was reuiu'd, and ioyd much in his semblance glad

on the surface
your stamp of individuality
is what made it possible

you are an object
of obsession and attraction
a dreadful secret
an indispensable pivot

Reason Why

even the doctor says
you need to lose a few pounds
to hit your ideal weight *(for your height)*

                                    that she to hunt the beast first

so add that to your list

            ("a battle to be fought or a victory to be won in
            establishing a dominion of self over self, modelled
            after domestic or political authority")

contest this abductor
chastise this *linea alba*
confer noblesse oblique here

And weigh the winde, that vnder heauen doth blow;
Or weigh the light, that in the East doth rise;
Or weigh the thought, that from mans [sic] mind doth flow.
But if the weight of these thou canst not show,
Weigh but one word which from thy lips doth fall.

your Cristalle Gloss in cappuccino rouge
looks real today, wow can hardly tell you're wearing
too bad the blow job smear
supposed to last all day

the word that falls is memory
unfortunately you have forgotten the details
of the thing that gives pleasure

(rules for everyday life)

jurisdiction over fold of belly
lies here, come lie here
join the community of ragged ovaries
penetrate the industrial region of tipped uterus
don't ignore outlying areas
just because there's no fire protection

or it's your turn to clean up first

take thy ballaunce, if thou be so wise

hit the beach
with these tools in hand

brighter than any other

        ("not a question of determining the 'working days' of
        sexual pleasures. . . but how to best calculate the
        opportune times and the
        appropriate frequencies")

sand sticks to everything
but the beach is all pleasure
except for the blackberry

schedule your performance review
for late in the day

        For no meanes the false will with the truth be wayd

wear something powerful
something slimming
show you're serious

the right time
correlation between variable states
and changing proprieties

you are a shift of emphasis
a delicate point
the most subtle form of austerity

These Counterfeits

weigh in the domestic realm
heavy with your domain
name your price to lock in

              (leave at your improbable peril)

transgression is expensive

try to triumph over
your *limited understanding*
fit into that suit

            (there is some necessity in "prolonging this conjunction")

stop generating contradictions
your left breast betrays you
being slightly larger than the right

And maske her wounded mind, both did and sayd
Full many things doubtfull to be wayd

mark out your perilous space
safe from censure still your wrist aches
awaiting your opportune moment
weighing the risk of inertia

(caught entropic by "twofold contribution")

the soft flow of blood
huge release: the gig's up

mental agility has compromised you again
can't you accept things
do you have to analyze everything
just buy your bed in a bag

values derided, ah, or, elided again
you mistrust your pleasure
justify your blame

She at her ran with all her force and might,
All flaming with reuenge and furious despight

who would be jealous of your bulging waist
as you traverse some poetic landscape
awaiting a rapturous response to your many stories

what is your role in the paradigm being portrayed
the etymology of your angry vocalizations
you fucking idiot
you repetitive dick

That womanish complaints she did represse
And tempred for the time her present heauinesse

careful: you're sewing a complex sexual tapestry
knitting a dilemma
cross stitching pornography
weaving a complex web
like Penelope: you could be up all night

           ("there is no right age for attending to oneself")

a newborn baby called "Marcus Aurelius"
and the door closes, slams shut

your flux will never swell so again
your uterus is your own

you are intensification of value
a widespread imperative
your reason is assigned
a doubtful mode

Bay

1. Horseshoe

hit the space of the side street
grass between toes
cherry dogwood blowing blossoms underfoot
cold pavement shivers the delicate undulation
your heel striking hard jolts tell your body
where you are almost the place you know best
see the street through the motion of your feet walking
where you stop pet the dog on chatham turn back
call the kids for dinner at the tennis courts feel the ground
linger as the basketball bounces grab and shoot

               line

                   lingers

                         (bp wrote)

red pier
like line
to sea

wave water taxi, wave today!

red bench too
wait like ellipse
ferries click into shore

turn not knowing who the you is
or should be

Spenser writes Great *Venus,* Queene of beautie and grace
but you are obsessed with the curve of the bay though
as a girl you were ambivalent about horses

2. Lions

back pressed into the heat of sand
you drink beer at the beach eat cool sushi
watch the boys jump off logs listen to conversations
fade to a dull growl

consider the beach your social map
some people w/ elaborate blankets massive baskets
some people are just the best at it
some people with thin towels pressed into a log
some people with macrame bathing suits
some people wear wet T-shirts

consider the beach your body's map
what you could have done all winter
refuses to fold back into its original shape

some people don't care

consider the beach your neighbourhood
you know it best
you know who belongs
you have cleaned up this beach
so others can leave their trash lying around? you don't think so
you are not afraid to say

consider the beach a private club, put up a sign saying "members only"
tell everyone it's so tour buses don't stop here
tell them "of course it doesn't apply to *you, you* are always welcome *here*"

3. English

you eat cupcakes on the beach during the day
drink peach schnapps at night under the stars
you think it's a glorious place on vacation from Calgary
you love rollerbladers in sleek spandex
you love watching people do yoga on the beach
you wear sunglasses even when it's raining pull your
fleece jacket close when the wind blows and everyone
else has left the beach for the day

you stay at the Slyvia (obviously!) write new notes
everyday at 6 a.m. the sun glinting pink off water off glass
you kick off your shoes (playfully) walk through sand until
your calfs ache with the effort and you think about renting rollerblades
yourself how hard could it be, go shopping for colourful yoga mats
to take home to all your friends, a Lululemon tank top tucked into
your jeans

4. Magna

you cut hair because there are no jobs for women here
open a salon in the basement your husband built for you
make a sign yourself, tell your friends, pin up flyers at the market
while the kids are at school

you love the beach, the boat, the little cabin across the street
fix it up to rent out in the summer, you love the boys, obviously,
your husband most of the time, your hair and even the imperfections
of your bikini clad body you love your life mostly

when it happens you think of neon flickering on your trip to
Las Vegas because it seems distant even though you can see
through the window in the cabin clearly what's happening
although it doesn't occur to you to hate him yet

such a fucking cliché you could easily kick her ass
but lately you're too tired to care that much
when the dog gets hit by the school bus though
you scream and cry until two in the morning when an infomercial
spray on cure for male balding calms you down

you walk the beach every morning to clear your head
smoke as you go leaving butts in your wake who fucking cares
drink coffee all day when you get back with milk but no sugar
cut a few heads of hair handing over magazines refusing to chat

5. Blind

your television broke and your dad wouldn't fix it
we swam in our underwear like brother and sister
do you think now we were given too much freedom
left alone while our parents drank rye and water
played cards laughed listened to the collection of country
records your mom won by phoning into CJFM

why don't we talk more

we knew so well how to be kids together

never imagined a future
where my kids don't even know your kids
we never drink rye rarely play cards can't stand country music

only see each other during some parental event
your dad dies
my parents stay married for 50 years
everyone takes our picture remembering (   ) from when we were kids

a poet I know wrote "the structure I hate also hates me, but it makes
me, and that's where the problem starts" but I wonder if the structure
that made us loved the idea of us too much for us to continue:
the structure keeps us here (   ) perfect dog-eared snapshot

6. Sannick

today this bay brings out my endless irritation with you
so much like married sex which leaves the seductive act
of undressing out of the equation in the hurry to get to the end
shrinking the middle into nothing

    (this is supposed to be epic, yep)

     I miss her
     I have missed her
     her I have never met

my tongue around a nipple
my tongue stuck in a pop bottle
wouldn't know what to say

bacon/eggs/fried scone served
blonde girl sun burnt red
one sunny day on the bay

tomorrow it will rain again, that's for sure
we'll stay in bed reading your snoring will have kept me up
later you'll strike conversations with strangers, but not if I'm there
regale me with the man from Stronach you could barely understand

finally after sending a postcard of a baby cow to the kids
I'll decide to stay again because how will it work otherwise
how do you transform longing into belonging, again?
you're so good at it fingers running through thinning hair

7. Moreton

you've never even been there, get off it
although you've heard the song about the convicts
a particularly difficult warden, life of misery
sung on a drive past looking out as the bay whips past

"To Moreton Bay I have found no equal
Excessive tyranny each day prevails"

Australians don't like to discuss this aspect of history much
I've noticed it fascinates the rest of us: so British so Irish most people
came for work later making the choice between Australia and Canada
sometimes by merely flipping a coin leaving "everyone" behind

"They stole me from my aged parents
And the maiden I do adore" he sings voice reaching folkish lament
the car stops a red light the "other" side of the road he looks over
makes sure I'm listening, it's important that he show me the bay
in just the right light, later we'll stop eat steak drink beer in tall glasses

we could be in Vancouver, Toronto but for the folk song

Queen(e)sland

A Brisbane Poem

dawn is a hazy light
I don't always get to see
suffuse with the blush on the palms
of the sun slowly rising
here on the other side of the earth
earlier the southern cross
emerged as clouds pushed past
hello scorpio's vivid immensity
across a dark sky rushing
along the river
to get to where we always end up
not home, but welcome
not altogether free, but wanting
to capture what's in front of us
that will someday be far away
leaning up into a different night sky
a glimpse back
arms out spinning

Fortitude Valley

one end of Brunswick to the next
marks the difference
whatever time
of day and especially night
RG as a beacon in the middle
people walking pass
on the left I'm finding
myself slightly out of synch:
outsider wanting to get
in deep somehow

                    no biking, no rollerblading, no skateboarding
                    no through road
                    no parking here

where Irish meets Chinese
on signs at least
a boarded-over don't tell ma
ma speaks enough languages
to justify the architecture
splitting beautifully amid
the mall at the centre
sipping coffee on the sidewalk
or sleeping in an abandoned alcove
while burly security patrols
                                no pick ups
                                no stopping
                                no left turn

a couple asks is this central station
no it's Brunswick I tell them thinking

people asking me where to go a
good sign of fitting in
although my accent might
have been a surprise
walking toward Ann Street a hand slips
behind my back to push the traffic light
a four-year-old with a blonde mohawk
held back by his dad until the light changes

                    no trainspotting
                    no waving
                    no stepping past yellow lines

McWhirters emerges like a mirage
but wait
it's apartments now people
always want to live where the action is
without the noise, though
techno lights exude prosperity
or a certain expansive urban style
granite countertop slick with
sleek stainless steel appliances
imagine your hip self there

                    no yuppies
                    no hippies
                    no two-tone streaks

galleries push up against prostitutes
garish colours blurring the bitumen
wicked vans or giant disco balls light
the night sky streets packed with people
at 3 a.m. eating pizza walking balconies

jammed music still reeling and good luck
getting a taxi tonight the zoo
raucuous jostling to dance backstage
enscribing your version on Ann Street
sensational standout for one night only

                                        no place to go
                                        except by 3 a.m.
                                        no entry after
                                        no entry

valley club boxers the toughest
in the world valley swimmers pull
kick glide faster than anyone
on Brunswick a man yells you fucking bitch
you fucking fucking bitch people pass
without stopping or turning to look
a Brisbane city brochure describes
the "colourful characters" in a precinct where
music remarkably takes precedent over
people who have just moved in
                              no smooth sameness
                              no montone
                              no monochrome, no

North Queensland Lustre

Queensland presents itself
in flickers
but also in bold gestures
bright green cane
audacious burning
fluffy white smoke
until water starved trees
break the monotony
of such relentless beauty

sugar cane as far as
reminds you of wheat
fields Saskatchewan shimmer green

                        there are a number of ways to be happy

Bundaberg blurs a motor
inn late in the hazy light
while Rockhampton waits
for a criterion steak searing
the old towers over as the new
tries to emerge in a place where
ghosts prevail and dance around
a ballroom where words bounce finely
tuned idioms off a crinkling chandelier

decorative iron grating punctuates
every view captured for later

                        places remember you
                        you remember photos

in Rocky the old palpably beats refuses
to let the slick stick shaking off
neon in favour of good hard wood
white washed or bare ghosts
shattering at every corner
capturing and holding what was
always theirs to rest for a second
the heat swelters beneath a tall column
or hide under a worn out bench

                        nostalgia lurks behind the tar black
                        wheel of every tractor passed

Townsville surprises as it rises
against the strand sprawling
to reach distant libraries where
readings are deadly good pushing
the quiet sense of place loud
bursting, but conciliatory such
power the edge of a chair pulled
close, but don't be offended, okay she says

music is the fourth companion
the fifth as Patti Smith levers
us out of each town into the open road

ocean hits the back of your eyes
coral sea blasts its salty air into
the top of your nostrils looking out
gasp as you snap more pictures

94

perched precariously on the side
lucky they didn't let you drive

                                               collect place names, creek signs
                                               count iconic kangaroos dead or alive

Cairns emerges bright and serious
but lights everywhere seem frivolous
like any tourist town careens amid
backpackers reminds you of Banff
swim the lagoon flattened against
the ocean cold breeze as the birds chirp
in the rainforest casino and jelly babies
pop out of the hazy lawn plump and jute
across from a white pillared library packed full
but the reef, even in the pouring rain stings
bright pictures into your mind

North Queensland flickers
radiant lustre
passing by

Outback Wanderlust

Longreach reaches into the base of my spine
to pull out all the misconceptions of the outback
like dark trees against vibrant skies
although there is that

the expansive view reaches beyond
where my hands can point pull back
the endless inches of sky and keep
it quiet here in my Saskatchewan
prairie born body

water whispers the landscape
the conversation the immense
blessing of rain making a green patch
beneath my blue shoes and a look of relief
in the corner of everyone's eye we pass

what a great place to be a kid
roaming free for all the days
until you go to boarding school
in Toowoomba when your life must become
regulated in a completely different way

red dirt still pushes up patterns
and holes the skin of this earth pitted
and perfect and so red
edges at the seams of my jeans

kangaroos don't fare well here
on the highway where road trains
push past fast bull bars ready to take out
whatever's in the way without stopping
thick tails hanging off the edge of the road,
heads removed vividly from bodies

verandas are everywhere in NOGO
sleeping outside mandatory when it's hot:
that old joke "it's 40 degrees in the shade
and there is no shade" but tonight the air
is pure chill my earlobes tingle
at the edge of the blankets

laughing from deep in my chest
around a fire burning but
political readings leave
my brain buzzing with connections
synapses firing in sympathetic visions,
the relief of colours exploring
the black parts of my mind

if you look up the stars are so vivid
you can feel the tilt of the earth,
the roundness of the spot on which
you are sitting head back you are
drowning in the Milky Way

History of
Sexuality

if you could deploy your indiscresive thoughts would that take you on a motorbike end of your hair whipping in the wind as you held tightly to a trim but growing waist if you followed that image across the Coquihalla Highway above Merritt glancing back to see the view below your leather clad arms grasping that leather clad waist of the one you've known but hardly ever risked if you could would you go for that ride east of Calgary toward Bragg Creek go camping for the weekend drinking and laughing with friends of friends instead of staying in a black and white bungalow mediating relationship issues and ignoring the phone when it rings if you lived out your repressive hypothesis would the imperative lie in running your fingers through dark curls looking reassuringly at big eyes wise to produce the twofold effect of overseeing control and suppressing the intensity of confession to rush through the days as they stack up noted and checked off on the surfer's paradise calendar without notating the perpetual spirals of power and pleasure, but instead capturing the beauty of mutual domesticity with papers dutifully stacked and hardwood floors artfully swept/polished with water and vinegar the scent your scintilla if you sought symmetry and reciprocity it's not hard to see when the problems become centred a pile from which you could build a ladder to the stigmata making a mess on the carpet or parapet on which you perch yourself to look out beyond the sound catalogue to the true love of the ocean whose erotics you have never ever questioned as an art of give and take because it's obvious who should yield you have never found yourself in a competitive situation tied directly to your ability to give pleasure never embraced the concept of duty at all really why would your body be tied to someone else's self worth would never again stake this civic status as a point of social negotiation because the state does implicate itself in the bedroom contrary to Trudeau's wishes bureaucracy gnawing at the edge of frayed sheets eager to bestow some privilege or legitimate results into little robotic citizens metal scraping the door jamb you believe in the Roman banquet shared by gluttony, drunkenness, and love: of course pleasure in food is linked to pleasure in sex to pleasure in alcohol and denial is the Christian concept you have been forced to embrace in order to make yourself sexually attractive you starve and disconnect your pleasure via this cultural ideology yet it is laid out in front of you all the time, side-by-side, impossibly skinny model next to fabulous bottle of wine, recipes at the back it's all stuff you can buy without thinking too much who wants to be Roman-huge anyway the care of the self is not a concept you can embrace clearly because the care of yourself is always tied to the care of other selves who are your responsibility the monuments to your audacity to think you could have it all like the feminists suggested and you're not blaming the feminists as is the current fashion especially among the younger generation to make fun of mothers who left copies of Kate Millett's *Sexual Politics* lying around their bedrooms or mothers who left condoms in drawers to provide opportunities for sexual liberation without painful consequences how hard for the children of feminists to rebel in lavish weddings in statements like he makes me whole with the body of a boy you threw your hood up and looked askance if anyone suggested otherwise refusing the cultural meaning of anything like a dress presenting the body in seven-year-old flux: boy/girl as needed stranding dolls in trees if necessary tossing apples and breaking plastic baby carriages right up until the point you were forced to decide or you intuitively realized it wasn't okay to hold hands or wrestle with your best friend in the playground that you were being watched and judged no one had to say anything

Acknowledgements

Thank you to the State Government of Queensland for a fantastic three-month residency in Brisbane which created time and space to complete this book (among many other things). Thanks especially to the incomparable Matt Foley whose passion for poetry permeates all aspects of his life and everyone else's around him. Thanks to Graham Nunn, Jules Beveridge, Michael and Sara Beaumont-Connop, Mick Richards, Martin Buzacott, Karen Hands, Merryon Ryall and Queensland Writers Centre folks, everyone at the Judith Wright Centre of Contemporary Arts, speedpoets, and friends all along the way.

Thank you to Michael Holmes for believing in my body of work, to Meredith Quartermain for much needed reading/suggesting/editing, Fred Wah, Peter Quartermain, Ashok Mathur and Aaron Peck. Thanks to Dr. Ron Bond (University of Calgary) for bringing Spenser so vividly to my attention in the first place. Thanks always to Heather Fitzgerald and Karen Robinson. Thanks to my family in Chase.

To B3: Bill, Brennan, and Blake thanks for living with me and without me, thanks for great stories, impressions, and dance moves. Thanks for all the loving support for me, and for the idea and adventure of poetry.